The BROKEN PIECES Of Me

Kimbria NiCole

The Broken Pieces of Me

Copyright © 2020 by Kimbria NiCole. All rights reserved. Printed in the United States of America.

Photo Credits: Jayden Meeks
Cover Art: Zavian Clayton
Edited By: Kimbria NiCole

ISBN: 978-1-71681-570-6

No part of this book may be reproduced or transmitted in any form by any means, graphic, electronic, or mechanical, including photocopying, recording, taping, or by any information storage retrieval system without written permission from the copyright owner except for the use of brief quotations embodied in a book review.

All scriptures are taken from the *English Standard Version* of the Bible.

Note:
The content within this book is for general informational purposes only as the author's personal thoughts.

In loving memory of Rev. Elaine R. Westbrook

> "Minister"
>
> KimBria
>
> Words are inadequate to express my appreciation and my love. You Are a God-Sent Child and I thank Him for you! Until you take on your own Project -- Keep on Spell-checking.
>
> Love,
> Mom

Words from my Mother - 2003

Dedication

I dedicate this book to my children, Marika, Zavian, and Jayden, who have journeyed with me throughout the past 24 years of my life. You have each experienced major pieces of my life including marriage, divorce, childbirth, abuse, grief, ministry, college, etc. Along with God, you have been the one constant throughout all my ups and downs and I truly cherish every moment of joy and sadness that we have shared. I want each of you to know that there is nothing that you can't overcome with God on your side. I love you!

To my husband, Harmon (Jr) and my bonus children, Leviticus (Dray) and Majuria (Moo Moo), thank you for choosing to love me, even on my worst day.

To everyone whom God has allowed to touch any part of my life: my parents, siblings, family, friends, and acquaintances. I honor each one of you for your love and support over the years. You may have come into my life for a season, some came for a reason, but I especially thank those of you who have been with me for a lifetime.

Thank you for loving every broken piece of me!

Table Of Contents

Introduction 7

Chapter 1: Broken Home 11

Chapter 2: Broken Heart 20

Chapter 3: Broken Trust 30

Chapter 4: Broken Chain 37

Chapter 5: Broken Speech 45

Chapter 6: Broken Wing 54

Chapter 7: Broken Spirit 65

God Uses Broken People 74

Scriptures on Brokenness.. 81

Introduction

It was during the worldwide COVID-19 shutdown that God began to deal with the many broken areas of my life. I was at a point where I was tired of accepting the way that I'd been for so many years, but I didn't quite know how to speak to the issues surrounding it. I often found myself struggling with expressing my true feelings about important matters, therefore causing me to conform, rather than to transform.

As an adult, I've allowed myself to be put in some very challenging positions. It's like I was more concerned about how others would feel versus how I would feel if I spoke up or made decisions that benefitted me. I chose to be passive over being assertive, which wasn't always the best way to deal with the situation. However, I now realize that being assertive is not about being confrontational, but more about standing my ground on what I believe.

Being passive recently cost me an opportunity for promotion on my job. Because I wasn't upfront and honest about how I felt about certain issues in my current position, I was considered underdeveloped and not quite ready for the next level. The sad part was that I knew that this was true. I realize that I tend to allow people to think that everything is alright when it's not, which is not fair to other people. I developed a bad habit of saying "I'm ok!" even when I knew that I wasn't. And that was not a good look for me.

When God released me to write this book, all I could think about was how I didn't want to air my dirty laundry just to be judged and criticized. Another hurdle I was trying to cross was how to tell my story without spilling somebody else's business. After sharing this thought with a friend and sister in Christ, she told me to pray about what I needed to say and trust God to do the rest. With that being said, I pulled out my pen and pad and started writing from my heart.

Although several people from my past and present have played a critical role in the creation of this book, it is not my intention to make anyone look bad in the eyes of the reader. However, I do desire to share the lessons that I have learned from my past hurts and shame. I truly believe that everything that God allowed me to go through was all a part of His plan and that He already knew that it would be necessary in order to help someone else to pick up their broken pieces and move forward with confidence.

Let's be honest, we have all had our fair share of unresolved issues, and sometimes we just need to know that we're not alone in this walk. Well, my brothers and sisters, I'm here to tell you that with God, you're never alone! I pray that this book will bring healing, self-acceptance, inner peace, restoration, deliverance, and a breakthrough for your heart, mind, and soul. Just know if God can deliver me from my mess, then He can definitely do the same for you.

Open your heart and your mind as you journey with me through my brokenness in hopes of helping you to get to that place of freedom and healing. The number one key to your deliverance is moving self out of the way and allowing God to have full reign over your life. That's important! You must be willing to let Him in. God simply sent me here to tell you that it's the broken pieces that make you who you are and that you can still be made whole from your broken pieces!

Chapter One

BROKEN HOME

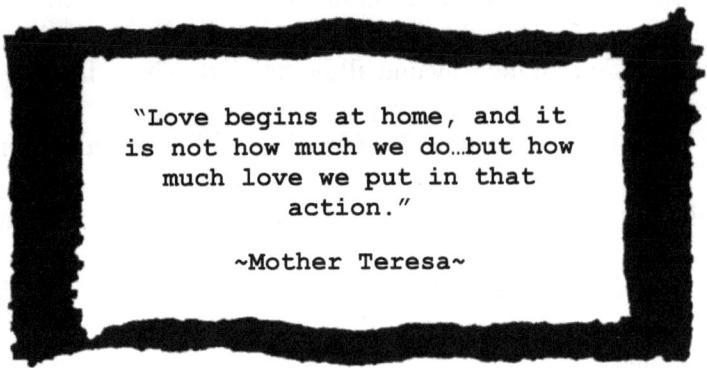

"Love begins at home, and it is not how much we do...but how much love we put in that action."

~Mother Teresa~

We've all heard the expression, "It begins at home." I believe this statement is self-explanatory, but allow me to elaborate a bit. What this is saying is that most of what we have learned stems from our early childhood teachings, which are usually taught in the home. We mostly hear this expression when it comes to dealing with ill-mannered children who suffer from a lack of structure and discipline, so they end up carrying those learned negative behaviors into adulthood. And because many of us consider home to be our primary foundation, we tend to believe that every learned behavior, positive or negative, begins at home.

Every child's first experience of love, validation, and acceptance comes from their home life. Whether they grew up with the sweet fragrance of "*I love you's*" casually swaying through the house, or they survived the disheartening effects of rejection through neglect and abuse, they learned how to give and receive love from what they saw at home. Maybe you were blessed to come from an upbringing where every day with your family was like a fun day at the park, while others came from a home where life's challenges got the best of the household. Either way, most of us have learned how to cope with life's ups and downs from the teachings and life lessons of someone in the home. Good, bad, or indifferent… it begins at home.

Unfortunately, today's norm appears to be a direct reflection of the products of our broken environment. It's relatively normal to have single-parent or blended family homes as our main foundation.

As I reflect on my foundation, I frown at the fact that I came from the societal norm of a single-parent home. My parents divorced when I was too young to ever remember them being married. My grandparents on both sides, remained married until they passed away, but they all lived separately throughout most of my life. As a result, I didn't have the luxury of having those positive marital examples to glean from. I was left to figure it out on my own.

Growing up, I mostly saw dominant, independent women playing the role of both parents while raising sons and daughters to become decent adults. I had my mother, my grandmothers, and my aunts, with a few encounters from my father and grandfather to watch and to learn from. Sad to say, I felt robbed of the opportunity to experience the protection and provision that should have come from having my father and grandfathers more active in my life. Yes, I did have my uncles, cousins, and brothers around, but it just wasn't the same. In my mind, there is an importance to being able to say "I'm gon' tell my daddy on you!" I didn't realize at that time that this issue was shaping and molding me into the independent person that I would soon become.

Although most of my family members played a part in my life, it was my mother who had the most influential impact. While I had the esteemed pleasure of watching her live out the ins and outs of her life in front of me, I had no idea that she was teaching me what and what not to do through her daily interactions. I must admit, there were many things that I saw as a child that made absolutely no sense to me, but it now appears to be clear to me as an adult. For instance, my mom's parenting style was so over-the-top as a child that my inner thoughts were elated at the idea of getting grown and being able to do whatever I wanted to do, or so I thought!

It wasn't long before I learned the difference between coming of age and being *grown*. Somebody should have told me that age was nothing but a number! I quickly came to realize that being an adult was not as easy nor as fun as I thought it would be. Once I started paying bills, struggling in relationships, and having children of my own, I would often catch myself singing these lyrics by hip hop artist, Ahmad:

"Back in the day when I was young, I'm not a kid anymore.

But some days I sit and wish I was a kid again."

I can actually appreciate what my mother was trying to accomplish as a single mother with multiple children and I've grown to respect every pointless rule that she had. Who knew that each rule would be necessary? Who knew???

My mom was fortunate enough to come up in a two-parent home. Unfortunately, functioning in dysfunction was their norm. She grew up in the heart of South Memphis, along with most of her other eleven siblings, but she was so determined to break that cycle of dysfunction that she did what she felt was necessary to make life better for all of us. My single mother fought to give my brothers and me the best life that she could give us, on her own. And even when we gravitated to that *other* way of life – mainly because we had so much fun – she refused to allow that to shape who we were.

I was an only girl with three brothers, and that made me feel like I had no choice but to be strong. I always felt like I had to prove my strength to those around me. Watching most of the women in my family was something like looking at Superwoman because they could do it all without missing a beat. So naturally, I felt that I had to be just as good as or even better than they were. Little did I know I was only setting myself up for failure because I didn't realize the danger in repeating the cycles of unrecognized brokenness. I was mimicking what I thought were the characteristics of strength and endurance, but in all actuality, they were more so fragments of unresolved issues, bitterness, guilt, hurt, and shame. I unknowingly learned how to be perfectly broken.

I had mastered the art of being broken so well that every time I would tell my stories of abuse and mistreatment, the response would always be, "Girl, you need to write a book!" At first, I shunned the idea because everybody has a story to tell. Everybody has endured some level of hurt and pain. What made my story so different that it should be in a book? It wasn't until I heard someone say, "Your testimony could be the very key to somebody's deliverance." At that moment, I decided, instead of telling my story from a victimized viewpoint, I would tell it from a survivor's standpoint! That way, I could help someone to survive their journey just by sharing a piece of my journey!

I believe God allowed me to witness firsthand what He was doing in my mom's life for such a time as this. I was able to see her win battles that the enemy tried to rig. He was crafty, but he never had what it took to take her out. She may not have lived an easy life, but through it all, she stayed connected to God. And He fought those battles for her! The thing my mother understood was that as a single mother of four, she knew the only way that she could keep us safe from the destruction of the enemy was to turn to God and trust Him for the outcome. What she knew was that she wouldn't always be around to make sure we did what was right, but she knew a Man who would. So, when she introduced us to God, she saved our lives and gave us a fighting chance.

Although we didn't have both parents growing up in our house, my brothers and I wanted for nothing. We had everything that we needed and most of what we wanted. She took the time to introduce us to a different way of living and thinking. She taught us about black and white movies in a world of full-color television. We were introduced to unspoken African American names like Ethel Waters and Eddie Anderson in *Cabin in the Sky*, as well as the lives of five White sailors; Joseph, Francis, Albert, Madison, and George Sullivan, better known as *The Fighting Sullivans*. We made some great memories!

I came to realize that being connected to our mother put us right in line for God's favor. She not only prepared us for life, but she also went out of her way to give us what she did not have. She included love, discipline, structure, and life lessons that we would never forget. My mom wasn't perfect, but she didn't allow mediocrity to be her stopping point. She knew that if she trained us up in the way that we should go, then we would not depart from that training once trouble knocked at the door. Did we do everything right? "No!" We didn't even follow every rule to a tee. But because of that firm foundation that she instilled in us, we were able to keep going, even after she departed to be with the Lord.

My point for saying all of this was simply to say, although my mom's foundation was that of a broken home, she showed us what it was like to know a better way of life than what she had known. She taught us that we should never settle for the status quo. She showed us that there's so much more to life than becoming complacent in a dysfunctional environment simply out of fear of experiencing an unfamiliar place. Philippians 1:6 assures us that "He who began a good work in you will bring it to completion." God doesn't start something He can't finish! He started a good work in my mother, but He's going to bring it to completion in the generations to come. It starts at home!

Chapter Two

BROKEN HEART

"Sometimes good things fall apart so better things can fall together."

~Marilyn Monroe~

When we think about relationships, we automatically associate it with the intimate feelings that we hold in our hearts for the opposite sex. But relationships can include friendships, relatives, or simple associations by communication. Every relationship will not carry the same weight, but true relationships can cause a strain if it falls apart. Sometimes, when we're not whole within ourselves, we become so emotionally attached to people or things that we begin to place more value on it than we should. Then, it becomes unhealthy or toxic. Sad to say, some healthy relationships will have to fall apart before we can come to realize the importance of it. But once a relationship of that magnitude comes to an end, heartbreak is sure to follow. Most of us won't miss it until it's gone.

I didn't always understand the relationship that I had with my mother, but I valued it for what it was. There were so many things that I truly admired about her. She was beautiful, fashionable, intelligent, talented, and most of all, she loved God. But the one thing that I didn't hold in high regard was her perspective on relationships. I felt like she deserved so much more than the world was willing to give her. She was a hard worker, a creative genius, and did I mention that she was beautiful? She was everything any decent man could hope for, but unfortunately, her relationships never seemed to agree with her. They simply did not reflect the type of qualities that she possessed. As much as I refused to accept that fate for myself, once again I was setting myself up for failure. I fell right into this dismal dungeon of dysfunctional doom. And that was a pretty hard fall!

After multiple failed marriages and relational let-downs, I found myself resting on the "couch of shame" that many of us as African Americans refuse to surrender to. It's amazing how we will seek advice from and share our pity parties with everyone we come in contact with, even a stranger in a grocery store if they show enough interest. But the wisdom of a professional therapist is totally out of the question. "I don't need nobody telling me how to live my life!" Now, I beg to differ! We all need professional counsel sometimes. If we're not careful, we can become so blinded by our determination to succeed that we begin to defame our character and allow our hearts to become contaminated and driven by pure negativity. Simply put, we can become bitter!

The initial purpose of my counseling session wasn't because I felt that I needed help. Don't get me wrong, I was that person in denial too. I was advised to seek grief counseling due to the loss of my grandmother, my close neighbor friend, and my mom all within one year. But once I started my sessions, within the first few minutes of the conversation, the "grief" sessions quickly turned into eight weeks of behavioral sessions. I was told that I was actually handling the grief very well, but that I was grossly mishandling my self-worth. I not only learned that I was selling myself short, but I also learned that I was operating in a spirit of insanity. I was repeating the same cycle while expecting a different result. I learned that I was so infatuated with the idea of being in a relationship that I was settling for things that should have been non-negotiable. I became content with dating men who were physically and mentally abusive, or men who were legally unavailable. I was basically repeating a cycle that should have been broken a long time ago.

As much as I fought to avoid mimicking the cycle of the relational issues in my family, I found myself soaring right into the open bay just as they were pulling out of them. Yikes!!! I was following in the footsteps set before me, and picking up right where they'd left off. And the worst part was, to justify staying where I knew I never should have been, I often used the cop-out that no relationship was perfect and that everybody makes mistakes. The question then became "Why did I think that this type of behavior was good enough for me?" I couldn't answer that question because I honestly didn't know the answer.

The hardest thing for me to do was to admit that I was a huge part of my own problems, but I had to be real with myself. The physical abuse, sexual abuse, mental abuse, and worst of all, the self-abuse was sadly what I had accepted for my life. I was more responsible for my poor relationship choices than I'd realized. As much as I wanted to shift all the blame to everyone, but myself, it wasn't all on them. Most times, I saw what I needed to see on the front end, but I was hell-bent on doing it my way. But my way wasn't God's way. For years, my pride wouldn't allow me to admit that I was wrong. I needed to be made whole before I could even begin to be who God created me to be. I was independent, but I wasn't whole. Lord knows I wasn't prepared to be anybody's wife. I was barely fit to be anybody's friend.

Being independent caused me to move at my own pace at times when I should have been trusting God for my next move. I traded a life of peace in exchange for rejection, abuse, and resentment simply because I'd decided to take matters into my own hands. I had attached myself to brokenness on so many levels and had become consumed with trying to fix boys in grown men's bodies. Let me clarify! I was trying to repair some things that were broken long before I came along. The worst part of it all was that I was unknowingly ill-equipped to handle the job. I couldn't be an effective helpmate to any of them because I too was suffering from open wounds of my past. While I was functioning off of the old wives' tale of leaving wounds open and uncovered, apparently I'd missed the updated memo that wounds should be kept clean and covered in order to heal properly. I was no more healed than they were. In fact, it was like the blind trying to lead the blind. I was operating out of my blind spot and my vision was blurry. I simply wasn't ready!

Those who were close to me often wondered why I fought so hard to bring out the best in others while accepting less than the best for myself. I wasn't always inclined to walk away from the hurt until it became so hazardous to my health that I no longer had a choice but to choose me. Even then, I could never bring myself to seek revenge for any wrong that I felt was done to me. Yes, I was angry, but deep down, I knew that I could relate to their pain. I allowed it because I was somewhat like them on the inside. We were all longing for some form of companionship as a means of validation. I thought I needed to have someone around me to make me feel useful. It felt like an even trade until the trade-off was no longer even.

For years, I secretly struggled with a negative self-image and tried to hide it behind challenging relationships and friendships. This way, no one would notice how bad off I was by myself. When you're alone, who can you blame for your failures and mistakes? You're left to deal with your own issues and many of us don't want that responsibility. So we choose to dress it up and hide it behind that one thing that we do well in hopes of not being seen for who we really are. It's like an artist who hides their pain behind their talents. The temporary applause from the crowd during a performance drowns out the pains of their issues, at least for that moment. For me, it was seeking validation by overcompensating with kindness. I wanted to be liked by people. But what good is it to be liked by man, if God is not pleased with who you are??? We're like damaged children inside of these adult bodies just begging to get out! And God is saying, "Come to me, all who labor and are heavy laden, and I will give you rest." (Matthew 11:28).

My brothers and sisters, God has given us this quarantine time to reconnect with Him! This is not the time for contaminating our hearts by gossiping on the phone, binge-watching Netflix movies, and perusing through social media. There's work to be done! It's time out for walking comfortably in self-doubt and hopelessness! It's time out for believing what the world and our past have said about us over the years! It's time out for taking our brokenness by the horn and joyriding it like the bull that it is (pun intended). No longer will we believe that we are our past mistakes! We are not our failed relationships! Rehearsing that pain and nursing the scars from your past hurt ends today! It's time to stop playing the victim and time to start recognizing the victory! It's time to break free from that stinking thinking of the broken-hearted. It's one thing to be free, but it's something about being free indeed!!!

According to several scriptures in the Bible, God is said to be a jealous God! He wants a personal relationship with each one of us. It doesn't matter how badly you've messed up. It doesn't even matter how many times you've messed up. Just know that whatever God has willed for you to do will not become null and void just because you made a bad choice. As long as there's breath in your body, it's not too late to repent and to ask God to give you a clean heart and a renewed spirit. Trust Him with all your issues and begin to walk in the grace that He has created for you. God is never caught off guard when we mess up. He created all of us in His image, but too many of us have chosen to take on the image of this world. Repent and get free from the perception of man! It's never too late to trust God with your broken pieces! Pray this prayer with me:

> *"Father, I thank You for our relationship! I thank You for healing my broken heart and delivering me from my past mistakes and hurts. I thank You for chastising me for settling for less than what You have for me. I thank You for never giving up on me. Although it took some time, You knew that I was coming out with my hands up! I thank You for waiting on me when I didn't have sense enough to move faster than I did. Father, create in me a clean heart and renew a steadfast spirit within me. I pray that You will bring healing to my soul as I begin the process of freedom from my brokenness. I pray that this book will help me to look in the mirror and begin to see myself as You have created me and not as my worldly circumstance has attempted to create for me. It's in Jesus' name that I pray this prayer. It is so! Amen."*

Chapter Three

BROKEN TRUST

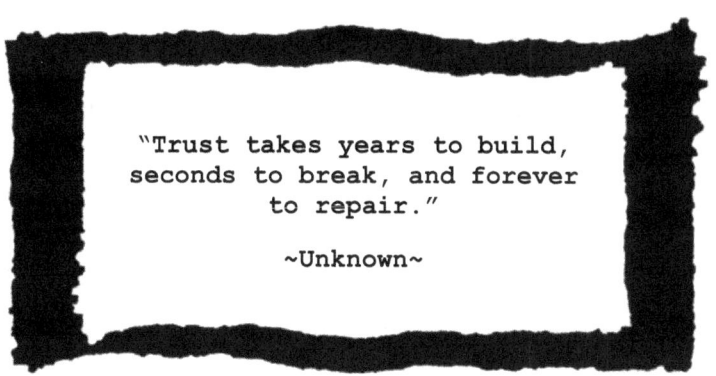

"Trust takes years to build, seconds to break, and forever to repair."

~Unknown~

Broken trust or betrayal holds a level of pain greater than most physical ailments. What's usually so sad about this is that it rarely comes from our enemies. This is true because the only way that betrayal can take place is through a breach of trust, which is usually built through the formation of a relationship. Many of us make the mistake of giving too much trust to those who render themselves untrustworthy, which often opens the door for betrayal. There's a very familiar passage of scripture that I consider to be one of the greatest formulas for trust, "Trust in the LORD with all your heart;

and lean not unto your own understanding. In all your ways acknowledge him, and he will direct your paths." (Proverbs 3:5-6).

It's a good feeling to be deemed trustworthy in the minds of others, but the truth is, none of us are perfect. We've all said or done something that may have caused someone's trust to waiver. Sometimes, the choices that we make simply cannot be reversed, and we end up paying for it for the rest of our lives. But ask yourself, "Was it even worth it?" The answer is probably "No!" Betrayal is never worth the consequence that's soon to follow. Broken trust is not easy to fix once the damage has been done. But the key to recovery is to face the music and accept the responsibility of your actions. Don't allow yourself to get stuck in that place of mistrust and cause it to rise up and take root in your life.

Betrayal and mistrust have had its playground since the beginning of time with what is coincidentally known in the Bible as *"The Fall."* Adam and Eve had broken God's trust by befriending a manipulative serpent with an eye-opening agenda. God had given clear instructions about NOT eating the fruit from the tree of the knowledge of good and evil. But while Eve was alone, she allowed herself to get set up and caught up, so she ate the fruit. Sometimes that's the danger of traveling alone. But anyway, she pulled Adam in on the scandal to take a bite as well. When they were confronted by God, Adam attempted to clear his name by putting it on Eve as the one who caused him to sin. It became the Old Testament version of the blame game. The problem is after so long, it begins to take on the effects of a landslide, quickly trickling down and causing devastation in other areas of our lives, as well as the lives of others. Ask me how I know? Don't judge me! But yes, I struggled with this one too. Just like Eve, many of us have gotten caught up in betrayal, which could have possibly cost us everything.

Doing what's right toward our brother seems like an easy task, but according to Romans 7:21, "When I want to do good, evil is always right there with me." Betrayal can become a never-ending cycle if we don't put a stop to it quickly. So, here's the landslide effect that I was speaking of. Cain, the firstborn son of Adam and Eve, betrayed his family by literally stabbing Abel, his younger brother, in the back. The weapon itself was never mentioned, but you get my point. Cain killed Abel. When God inquired about Abel's whereabouts, Cain responded with a question, "Am I my brother's keeper?" This is a question that I would like for you to think about for a moment. God did not create us as a community of believers who would only look out for themselves. We're here to fellowship and love one another as the body of Christ. "Behold, how good and how pleasant it is for brethren to dwell together in unity!" (Psalm 133:1). In order to stand united, we must strive to build relationships and refuse to kill them with broken trust. It's time to drop our hidden agendas in order to move forward!

Too many of us find a dwelling place in mistrust based on something that may have happened to us years ago. We build up these defensive walls with hopes of keeping people out, only to end up isolating ourselves from the world. Our mental residence becomes a place filled with what-ifs while allowing every negative thought to dominate our minds. This is just a trick of the enemy! His job is to steal, kill, and destroy the character and integrity of the people of God, by any means necessary. So, as God's disciples, we must be mindful and intentional about how we handle our God-given assignments. While many of us are taking a 15-minute break, Satan is forever on the clock fostering a climate of betrayal, deceit, and mistrust. It's time for us to clock back in and get back to work because he doesn't take a break.

We get hung up on the fact that we've been hurt before and have a greater fear of it happening again. Well, guess what? It will come up again, just in a different manner. You survived it then, but this time you'll be better prepared to survive it again. Because we live in a world full of joys and sorrows, we never can tell which one we will encounter today. That's why we can't keep giving in to the distractions of the enemy. He won't need a key or a cracked door to enter in. He's crafty enough to make his way in through the peephole if we stand at the door peeping long enough. He's divisive enough to even come in through the words that we speak. And because we are flawed, we're bound to speak out of turn at some point. The cycle will only get worse unless we take on the responsibility of breaking it. Tell yourself, "With God, what's broken can be mended, and what hurts can be healed."

I remember I used to think of every negative scenario that could possibly happen in my life. I thought every time someone passed away, whatever happened to them was bound to happen to me. I would try to figure out what they could have done to make God call them home at that particular time. If they had cancer, I feared that I would have cancer. If they suffered a heart attack, every beat of my heart was about to be my last. My goodness! Who wants to live like that? I allowed my lack of trust in God's provision to turn into fear. I had to start living in the scriptures and standing on the promises of God. 2 Timothy 1:7, "For God has not given us a spirit of fear, but of power and of love and of a sound mind" became my daily affirmation. This scripture got me through many dark nights. I had to make the decision to break that spirit of fear.

Although I learned that fear is simply "False Evidence Appearing Real," I allowed fear to cause me to lose trust in people and in situations. I allowed it to paralyze me and stop me dead in my tracks. Because I often failed to handle it properly, I believe it may have caused me to miss the mark on a few blessings that God had in store for me. The spirit of fear had delayed my progress. It was then that I realized that I was allowing my fear to outweigh my faith. Fear of rejection, fear of failure, and fear of the unknown had me too afraid to make a move, forward or backward. There were times when I could clearly hear Christian speaker, Joyce Meyer saying, "If you stand in the middle of the road long enough, you're bound to get hit by a car. JUST MOVE!!!" I learned to move, even with my knees knocking, and my heart pounding. Fear opened the door for mistrust, but I chose to ignore fear and to put my trust in God.

Chapter Four

BROKEN CHAIN

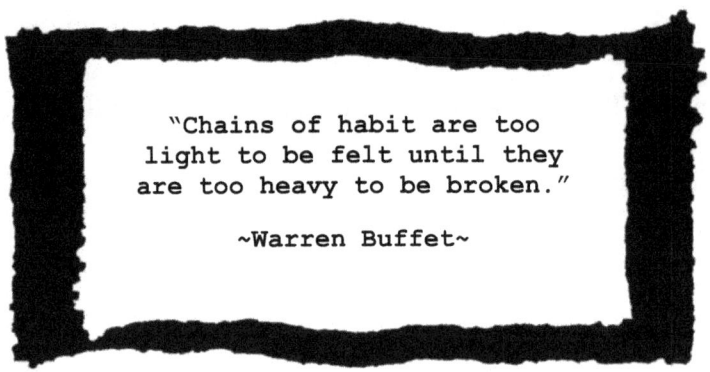

"Chains of habit are too light to be felt until they are too heavy to be broken."

~Warren Buffet~

Have you ever dealt with a person who could tell you every wrong turn that they've ever taken in life, but could never tell you where or when they finally went right? They could pinpoint exactly how, when, and where they got stuck, but couldn't tell you if they ever broke free. In fact, they would get stuck in the same repeat cycle, manage to get themselves out of it, only to get stuck in it again. That was me! It was a continuous cycle of dysfunctional bondage. I felt like I was bound by chains and didn't know how to break free. But after recalling the chain-breaking story of Paul and Silas when they were locked in jail, I realized that praise and worship was my way out! The chains may limit my praise, but no chain is strong enough to kill my worship! I was ready for God to break the chains!

For years, people spoke of their respect for my strength to go through the things that I had encountered, but not many people challenged me to take the necessary steps to break the cycle. They made excuses on my behalf about how it was never really my fault, and how I deserved so much better than what I'd gone through. But you would think that at some point I would have paid attention to the red flags and recognized the signs, especially since I was more familiar with them the third and fourth time around. What was it about me that made me feel that this was what I deserved when others around me felt the total opposite? Why did so many people accept my victim mentality rather than challenge my decision-making skills? That lack of challenge from myself and those who loved me unconditionally was just as crippling as my willingness to stay in bondage. Refusing to rebuke and challenge a person's broken state can be just as damaging as that person's failure to see what God has placed inside of them.

Sometimes, we love people in such a way that we think allowing them to be who they are without the challenge of doing better is the acceptable thing to do, but we're really doing them a huge disservice. Loving your brother with the love of God looks something like Hebrews 12:6, "For the Lord disciplines those he loves, and he punishes each one he accepts as his child." and Proverbs 3:12, "For the Lord corrects those he loves, just as a father corrects a child in whom he delights." So, if God deals with us through discipline and correction, why are we using this watered-down method for those who we're called to love? Imagine how many chains that could be broken if we would just show a little bit of that godly kind of love through rebuke, discipline, and chastisement instead of false justification and pacification just to maintain the peace.

My mom was one of the few who truly knew how bound I really was. She saw the damaging chains of the generational curse hanging from me like a cheap bulky necklace, slowly weighing me down. She recognized my lack of confidence and the secret need for validation when everyone else saw the tough girl/tomboy side of me. That was a recipe for relationship disaster! She saw the train wrecks that were about to come my way, but by the time I became an adult, there was only so much that she could do or say to reel me back in. If I can be completely transparent, a small part of me didn't want to listen to her advice as it related to dating because I secretly felt that due to her track record, she was in no position to advise me on best practices for my relationships. I saw us as complete opposites in this area and assumed that I knew what I needed way better than she did. What I soon came to realize was that she was in the **BEST** position to advise me. The fact that her past experiences didn't break her made her well qualified to speak to that very familiar spirit in me.

As fragile as my mom knew that I was, she also recognized the fighter in me. I believed in going hard for those I loved. But it wasn't until I experienced domestic abuse in my first marriage that I was no longer able to stand up for myself with confidence. I didn't know what it was to run, so I always stood ten toes down, and I went in. But as time went on, if I had to fight, I fought afraid. I just couldn't understand how the very one who claimed to love me so much could physically hurt me so bad. I knew that I could only take so much before I would privately crash. But God sustained me, and He had my back! God hasn't permitted me to put that testimony in writing, so I won't be including that in this book. Just know that by the acknowledgment of His voice and my willingness to be obedient, God spared my life. If it had not been for the AMAZING grace of God that saved a wretch like me, I wouldn't be here today! God covered me, and He kept me!

Excuse me while I praise Him!!! ***GLORY!!!***

For far too long, I suffered in silence from the after-effects of different forms of abuse. I allowed people to play with me just as they would a damaged toy. They could bend me, break me, and toss me to the side because I didn't demand the respect that I was expected to give. In my mind, I was already damaged goods, so I marked myself down as a cheap item on a clearance rack and settled for less. I didn't know my value at the time, but allow me to be the first to tell you that choosing to love yourself is never a selfish choice. In fact, in order to be fully capable of loving someone else, you must first know how to truly love yourself. That goes for all of us, male and female! Although no relationship is perfect, I had to stop lowering my standards to accommodate the imperfections and insecurities of others. People only do damage to others when they too are damaged! Simply put… hurt people only hurt people. It's time to gain the strength to stop allowing outside influences to dictate what your life should look like. That's not their job!

I remember waking up one morning around 5:30 am, recollecting words that I'd heard in a dream. It was like a light bulb had gone off and I realized that it was God affirming me. I'd heard it in my spirit, but needed to believe it in the natural. I heard God speak these words to me, *"My child, do not allow the guilt of finding yourself and letting go of what hurt you to make you feel ashamed. You are loved! You are forgiven! You are yet becoming who I created you to be! You do deserve better! Your past is in the past! You are so much more than you believe, but you will never see that if you refuse to open your eyes. You've become content with being pulled from nowhere to nowhere. I didn't create you for this! I created you for a specific purpose and I'm expecting you to walk boldly in it. My child, I saved you from a burning house as a teenager because I had a plan for you. I delivered you from that abusive marriage because I had work for you to do. I didn't stop loving you after that abortion, and I didn't turn away from you after that divorce. As unworthy as you felt, I forgave you because you needed to know that my love for you was unconditional. Now, hold your head up high and move forward… even on your broken pieces! Your chains have been BROKEN!!!*

After shedding tears of joy, I surrendered my will over to God. I'd wrestled with bad choices and played with my life long enough! It was time for me to put my next moves in His hands. It was beyond time for me to let go and let God! I had to put my past in the past and break that cycle! We claim to be so tired of the status quo, yet we continue to live as a statistic or stereotype. I had two choices - I could either stay in bondage, or I could choose to break out of those chains. The choice was mine. It was high time for those chains to come off!

To whoever needs to hear this… God says, ***"Your chains have been BROKEN!!!"***

Chapter Five

BROKEN SPEECH

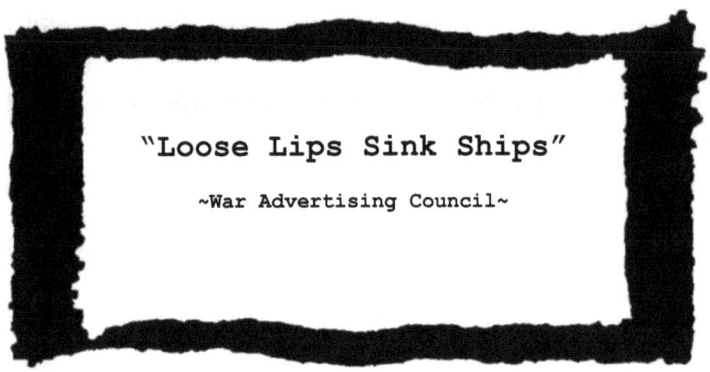

"Loose Lips Sink Ships"
~War Advertising Council~

In 1985, Run DMC released a song entitled, *You Talk Too Much*. The lyrics are not that deep, but they are profoundly descriptive of what causes many of us to stumble with our words. Some people are natural talkers and they simply love to talk, and then you have those who possess loose lips and random words just fall out every time they open their mouths. There's actually a difference. If you're talking about life and things in general without slandering someone's character, then you just might be a natural talker. But if you're *"carrying bones,"* as it's referred to in the urban vernacular, then you may be guilty of possessing loose lips. The song refers to people who talk a lot as instigators, orators, blabbermouths, etc. I'm thinking that this would be a perfect place for me to insert a *"You're stepping on my toes!"* Sometimes, the light of the truth exposes those dark places that we prefer to keep hidden. But I've learned that God can't use us to our fullest capacity if we're comfortable hiding in the dark.

God calls us to speak life over EVERY situation in order to enhance our life and the life of those assigned to us. But when we speak death, we chance to kill every living thing around us. Steve Harvey said it like this, "Stop killing people's character by giving legs to negative conversations concerning them!" He explained how negativity takes on a life of its own when you choose to carry it and spread it around loosely. It's only human to want to tell your side of a story or to just plain ole' gossip about things just because you have detailed information about it. We're aroused by the idea of knowledge being power, but truth be told, too much knowledge can become dangerous. Knowing something that someone else does not know may give you the advantage in that particular conversation, but it also allows you the opportunity to demonstrate self-control. I've had to learn this lesson the hard way on several occasions. I've spoken negative things about others that I'd later wished that I could take back, but unfortunately, I couldn't. I've repeated things that should not have been repeated and have had to pay mightily for it. I just believe that there comes a time when God expects us to GROW UP and to know when to SHUT UP!!!

There's a slogan that read, *"Loose Lips Sink Ships,"* on a public service ad during World War II. It was used to remind Americans of the dangers of revealing too much information to the enemy. This expression simply meant to beware of unguarded talk. I was right in the middle of completing this chapter when I heard those words somewhere in the background. I couldn't figure out if I'd heard this on a TV show or what, but I assumed God was trying to tell me something. Hmmm… With that being said, I did a little research on the slogan and I was both shocked and amazed at the correlation. Once again, God's timing was perfect! He sent just what I needed to hear at the time that I needed to hear it. This made me realize that I am solely responsible for how I handle negative information once it comes to me, and I've got to learn how to let the talking stop at me.

I didn't share this finding with anyone because as I said in the *Broken Chains* chapter, it's normal for your circle to love you to a point of pacification. Just as people will try to convince you that you're being too hard on yourself, God will let you know when you're out of order. Let me just say this… God was on point with this one! *"Loose Lips Sink Ships,"* allowed me to see that I had been guilty of sinking a couple of ships in my lifetime. Although it was nothing to be proud of, it was my truth. It may not have been malicious or intentional, but the fact still remains… the ships sank. In fact, they'd started sinking around me as fast as the "unsinkable" *Titanic*. I'd spoken out of turn and shared private information that proved to be detrimental in the end. I had to learn that having information did not always give me the green light to share that information. Sometimes, when we have something to say, we just have to say it to God and leave it with Him.

I truly believe that God was using this time of listening as an opportunity to keep speaking. I had another early morning encounter where He spoke again on this topic of over-talking. As I was tuning in for my daily 6:45 am prayer on the 95.7 Hallelujah Praise Party, the radio host opened with 1 Corinthians 13:11, "When I was a child, I spoke like a child, I thought like a child, I reasoned like a child. When I became a man, I gave up childish ways." He mentioned the importance of showing signs of maturity by not sharing all of your inward thoughts with everybody who's open to listening. After hearing this, as odd as it may sound, all I could think about was a wet sponge. Sometimes you encounter people who soak up negative information like a sponge. But remember this… sponges always leak when they're squeezed.

He went on to talk about how some things are better left unsaid in order to avoid the risk of ruining your future or the future of others by speaking negatively about them. He said that we should repent and then ask God to kill the seed of every negative crop that had been planted to keep them from growing and manifesting. That piece alone made me realize that my God is a God of divine restoration! Although I'd planted seeds of negativity, doubt, and strife, it wasn't too late for God to turn it into a season of harvest. His Will is to deliver us from all evil, even if the evil lies within the words that we speak. What Satan meant for evil, God is able and willing to turn it around for our good!

Satan desires to make a fool out of you and have you to believe that as long as what you're speaking holds an ounce of truth, then you're justified to speak it. This is so far from the truth! Always ask yourself if the words that you're about to speak will hurt or help the situation. If it's gossiping, backbiting, or lying, not only will it bring pain, but it also opens the door for self-destruction and witchcraft. But according to Psalm 107:20, "God has sent His Word [Jesus Christ] to heal us and deliver us out of all our destructions." He has also given us the power to speak life over dead situations, peace in the midst of a storm, and healing over our bodies. God has granted each of us the power to bring life or death in the things that we speak. If we're truly called to be our brother's keeper, then we're responsible for asking God to teach us how and when to speak concerning their lives.

Broken speech is a disability similar to that of a speech impediment. Just like a speech impediment, it affects our ability to speak properly. Many of us subconsciously suffer from a spiritual speech impediment. We speak out of turn, we speak negatively about others, and sometimes we're simply afraid to speak at all. In Exodus 4, God sent Moses to talk to Pharaoh about freeing the Israelites out of Egypt and Moses said, "I am slow of speech and tongue." God responds by telling Moses that He will help him to speak and teach him what to say. Simply put, God desires to heal us in every area, including our speech and He will never send us out unprepared. Who is He sending you to speak to?

Sometimes, we can't speak life because we're holding grudges against the one who God has sent us to speak to. There's a quote that says, "Harboring unforgiveness is like drinking poison and waiting for someone else to die." The same applies to speaking death. Some of us are dying a slow death trying to kill someone else with our negative words. We're holding people hostage in the house that they used to live in, even after they've moved into a new house in a totally different neighborhood. Once they've become settled in their new home, we've got to release them from where they used to live. They simply don't live there anymore. What am I saying? We've got to release people from where they once were and speak life into where they are now. Stop drinking from the poison and start drinking from the living water flowing in John 7:37, which was promised to anyone who's thirsty.

My desire is that this will help you just as it has helped me. In order to preserve your integrity, it is important that you have a plan of attack whenever you're presented with negative talk. My dad used to say "If you fail to plan, then you plan to fail." Because I didn't have a plan, over-talking took root and had become a part of my reputation, but it was never meant to be a part of my plan. So, if you find yourself getting caught up in those negative useless conversations, just remember the phrase, *"Loose Lips Sink Ships."* Hopefully, this will serve as a constant reminder for you to be careful when you speak, who you speak to, and what you speak about. Ask God, as David did in Psalm 141:3-4, "Take control of what I say, O Lord, and guard my lips. Don't let me drift toward evil or take part in acts of wickedness." And most importantly, ask Him to deliver you from the practice of being overly talkative, especially as it relates to carelessly revealing information that may be private or confidential. This may sound a bit harsh, but until you're able to master the ability to be quiet, just ask the Master to teach you when to SHUT UP! For the faint at heart… Shhhhh!!!

Chapter Six

BROKEN WING

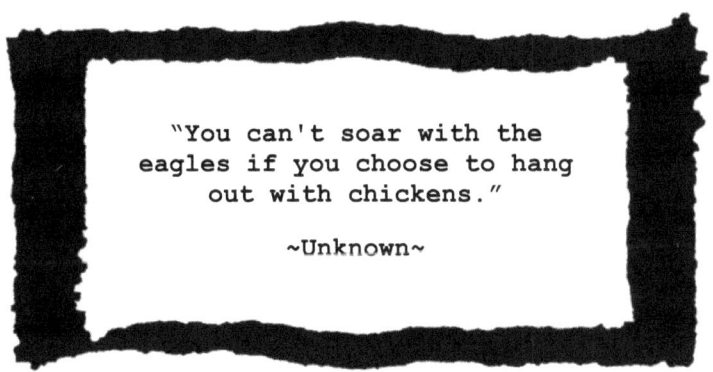

"You can't soar with the eagles if you choose to hang out with chickens."

~Unknown~

For years, I suffered from what's called broken-wing syndrome (BWS). This is a condition that describes a person who is often attracted to people in need, empathetic to people whom they can fix, or who expects the same level of love and loyalty to be fully reciprocated. This is basically how I was described by the counselor during my grief sessions about ten years ago. She deduced from our sessions that I'd always had a desire to date fixer-uppers in hopes that they would appreciate my efforts and return the same level of love. She also explained that it usually doesn't work out that way, but of course, I had to find that out the hard way.

Making myself available when I saw a need was like second nature to me. I enjoyed the feeling that came with being in a position to help, but I never realized that it came from a place of brokenness. Apparently, I had a compulsive need to be needed. No one could have made me believe that this was how I carried myself in hopes of feeling loved and appreciated. But as I look back over the years, it's more apparent now that I'm aware of what to look for. There were times when I would put myself in a bind just to make sure others were good. I thought to be selfless was a great attribute to have, but when it comes to picking others over yourself, it's no longer considered an attribute, but a form of self-sabotage. My *broken wing* wasn't seen by the natural eye as a visible scar, but more as a symbol of being spiritually torn or damaged, which limited my will to fly.

I read an excerpt from an article that talked about how broken wings can be very traumatizing for birds. In fact, a bird with a broken wing will likely feel more vulnerable and might lash out at you with its beak or claws, especially the wild ones that often depend on its flight for survival. Unlike a bird, our physical need to fly is not as critical, but the preparation is quite the same. A baby bird has to rely on its mother for protection and care until its wings are strong enough to fly on its own. And unfortunately for some of us, we have become content with relying on others to care for and carry us for far too long. The article also mentioned how a broken wing can slow down a bird's flight, setting them back temporarily. This can also be true as it pertains to people. When we suffer from issues of brokenness, it can be just as traumatic while making us feel vulnerable and slowing down our progress as well.

"Even youths grow tired and weary, and young men stumble and fall; but those who hope in the Lord will renew their strength. They will soar on wings like eagles; they will run and not grow weary, they will walk and not be faint" (Isaiah 40:30-31). If you become too complacent being carried or carrying people with *broken wings*, you will eventually hinder their opportunity to soar like an eagle. But get this… God wants all of us to soar! But how can you soar if you're forever relying on the push of others rather than the move of God? Yes, you may stumble and sometimes you will fall, but you can't get tired and give up on the promise that God has given to us to run without growing weary, or to walk without fainting. Even with a *broken wing*, or emotional scars, as the urban dictionary defines it, God can still use all of us to fly. But if we are afraid of heights, we will never get off the ground. God is calling us to flight!

Many of us are stuck on the notion that God can't use us if we have broken pieces or missing parts, but that's so far from the truth. God does not call those who are perfect, but He does call those whom He can perfect. He seeks those who are willing, even if they are a bit nervous. He seeks those who are willing to take up their spiritual cross and suffer as Christ suffered. He calls those who understand that being called does not always require four walls and a pulpit. God is no respecter of persons. Being called is simply being chosen by God to worship Him, to carry out His assignment, to obey His Word, to be intentional about living a life that's pleasing to Him, which means He can even call YOU! Just know that all callings aren't pretty or easy because it might require you to bear the pain of flapping your *broken wings* in order to fly!

    Sometimes, I would find myself trying to fly, but I would feel this constant tugging and pulling that wouldn't allow me to get too far off the ground. It was like being on a nonstop rollercoaster ride full of ups and downs. I believe the reason it wasn't as noticeable to others is because I hid behind my independence. Although I was independent, I was far from whole. I learned how to fake it in order to make it work for me. Go figure! I'd become comfortable dragging my baggage along the ground instead of pushing through the pain of soaring to new heights. I owed it to myself to learn that the true purpose of my wings was to take me new levels. It was beyond time for me to learn how to fly from my place of pain to my place of purpose.

When we think of pain, we tend to think of punishment. But God, sometimes allows us to experience the pains of life in order for us to appreciate our purpose in life. Think of it as a woman giving birth. Although the pain of childbirth can be somewhat unbearable, the purpose behind the pain is well worth it. There's a period of discomfort from the contractions and pushing that leads to a greater level of joy in the end. As a mother, I wouldn't trade that feeling for anything in the world! Similar to childbirth, God has placed a form of life called purpose, inside of each of us, and He expects us to bear the pain of bringing it to fruition, no matter what the cost. As gospel recording artists, Mary Mary said, *"Nobody told me that the road would be easy, but I don't believe He brought me this far to leave me."*

"Operation Broken-Wing" had taken up full residence in my life. I had become a slave to my cycle of brokenness and didn't know how to break free. I was loyal to those who were disloyal to me, but I was also guilty of being disloyal to those who tried to be loyal to me. I was an absolute mess, but I refused to give up! Being stuck in a rut was not the way that I wanted to live out the rest of my life. I realized I was slowly being pulled away from God and losing sight of myself. It was time for me to trust God to pick up my broken pieces and make me whole again. But until then, I had to push past the pain of my broken-wing syndrome so that I could fly as high as God would allow.

One day, as I was listening to my iHeart Radio 80's playlist, an old 1985 favorite of mine started to play. The song is entitled "Broken Wings." As many times as I'd heard this song throughout my life, it had never had this type of effect on me before. It was as if God was releasing me and setting me free. At that very moment,

I felt free to fly! The tears began to fall as I listened to what felt like God speaking directly to me through these lyrics:

"Take these broken wings,

And learn to fly again,

And learn to live so free.

When we hear the voices sing,

The book of love will open up,

And let us in.

Take these broken wings."

I was being released from the pain of past hurts, rejection, and betrayal. I was being released from the perception of people. I was being set free from the self-inflicted pain of divorce, abortion, gossiping, low self-esteem, and self-pity! God had taken my *broken wings* and taught me how to fly again! I'd spent so much time moving and trying to free myself, but God was just waiting for me to be still long enough to release me. The time in quarantine allowed me to do just that. He taught me how to love myself despite my past mistakes and failures. He taught me how to remain unstuck from the things that He'd already released me from.

Along with my release, I eventually had to inspect my circle and watch the company that I kept. Not only were some of them not good for me, but I also was not good for them. Some of us were enabling each other and not holding each other accountable for our actions. Everybody's not meant to be in your circle. It reminds me of the story where the eagle was being raised on the farm with a chicken. All he knew was to peck around on the ground like a chicken. But one day, the eagle saw another eagle flying high over the farm and he was amazed at how graceful and free the eagle was. He told the chicken that he wished that he could fly like the eagle, and the chicken told him that it was impossible because he was just a chicken and chickens don't fly. So, the eagle accepted that word and continued to live his life as a chicken, never realizing that he was equipped to fly just as high.

The moral of this story is God has equipped each of us with a measure of grace, and the freedom to fly, but if we never find out who we are, we will never leave the ground. It's not necessarily about knocking the chicken because they serve a purpose as well. My brothers and sisters, what words are you accepting contrary to what God is saying? God did not call you to be a chicken! He called you to be an eagle! Are you ready to fly like an eagle? What are you waiting for to soar? God sent me here to tell you that He has fixed your *broken wing* and He's ready for you to take flight!

Once you begin to walk in your God-given purpose, then you can receive the strength that you'll need to spread your wings and fly. No longer will you have to compare and compete with someone whose *wing* is just as damaged as yours. And at the same time, it's good to have the desire to want to help someone else, but it's dangerous when you're ill-equipped because you run the risk of making matters worse. God is in the restoration business! So let God be God! Let Him do the fixing! Let Him take your *broken wings* and teach you how to fly again, so that you can be free! The sky is literally the limit!!!

Chapter Seven

BROKEN SPIRIT

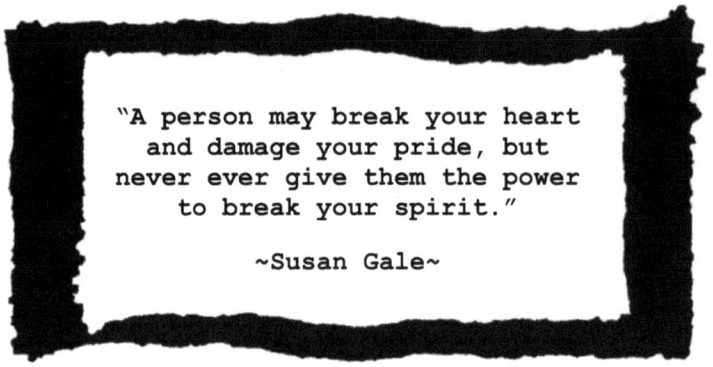

"A person may break your heart and damage your pride, but never ever give them the power to break your spirit."

~Susan Gale~

Dealing with life's issues allowed me to feel justified in celebrating the woes and emptiness of my broken spirit. No matter how much random people prayed for me, I just couldn't seem to shake the trials of my impaired self-image. I often struggled to grab ahold of the power that I knew was on the inside of me. I was operating off of the potential that others saw in me because I was secretly afraid to walk boldly in my purpose. Many would disagree with someone being in ministry while admitting that they're broken and afraid, but I knew that I was hand-picked by God to carry out this assignment.

So I no longer felt the need to be validated by the naysayers. I decided to just keep walking, knowing that God is walking with me.

Although I'd endured a lot of pain and hardship over the years, I had to learn how to thank God through it all. I found myself thanking Him for every up and every down, every damaged area of my life, every failed relationship, every heartbreak, every tear, every defeat, etc., because that's what made me who I am today. As painful as it was, I realized that I had to be exposed in order for my record to be expunged. Sometimes, exposure is the only true way to see the whole big picture. It wasn't always pretty, but it was all necessary. God had to show me who I was before He could empty me out and refill me with my true identity. He cleared my record and He changed my story!

I like to refer to this chapter of my life as my King David chapter. When we hear about King David's backstory, rarely do we hear about his issues and hang-ups first. We like to hang our hats on the fact that God referred to him as *"a man after His own heart!"*

We marvel at the idea of God choosing the scrawny insignificant kid over all of his more suitable brothers to be worthy of the sacred oil because it gives us a bit of hope. God saw something in David that David couldn't even see in himself. Like many of us, David didn't know his true identity. But God cleared his record and He changed his story!

Although David struggled greatly in the position that he was appointed to, God was not caught off guard by his questionable behavior and lack of integrity. He knew everything there was to know about David long before He sought after him, but He sent for him, nonetheless. Trust me, God is well aware of every secret broken place that we think we're hiding in our hearts, yet He still chooses to use us for His kingdom. Just like King David, we all have a backstory and we've all done unthinkable things in our appointed positions. But the most important principle that we can take from King David's experience was his ability to humble himself and repent.

His exposure was necessary because it's nearly impossible to operate successfully in the kingdom with covered secrets. We tend to get so lost in the hidden agendas that we lose sight of God's chosen path. Following my agenda caused me to lose some things along the way. One great loss was my peace of mind. I was losing it piece by piece with issues in my marriage, my children, my ministry, my friendships, my integrity, my finances, etc. I felt like I was literally falling apart. But because God won't put more on us than we can bear, He allowed me to endure the very things that should have taken me out or could have caused me to lose my mind.

God cares so much for our well-being that He not only allows us to experience difficult days and the hardship of our storms, but He grants us the gift of His presence during the storm. Contrary to the thought of the nonbeliever, God doesn't do anything to intentionally bring harm to His children without a plan of rescue and restoration. According to the popularly quoted scripture of Jeremiah 29:11, "He has a plan for our welfare and not for evil, to give us a future and a hope". The issues that we go through may not always look good, but God can surely turn it all around for our good! My brokenness was not purposed to be my end, but to show me that I can survive on the *BROKEN PIECES OF ME*!

I had no idea that I was broken in so many areas until I started writing and actually reading what I was writing. But I had to come to grips with the fact that all of this was necessary. There was absolutely no way that I could have received my healing if I'd never realized that I was ever broken. It's a hard pill to swallow when you no longer recognize the person you see in the mirror every day. I was accepting defeat in areas simply because I was too afraid to speak out. Something in me just wouldn't allow me to stand up. Saying "No" became darn near impossible. Have you ever noticed how a bobble-head just nods in agreement with everything? Well, that was me! I'd become a "Yes Man," simply to avoid conflict even when I disagreed. While I was trying not to rock the boat, God had given me permission to get out of the boat!

Allow me to take this time to share a simple message of hope with those who may know and understand this feeling all too well. After King David messed up, he cried out for God to create in him a clean heart and to renew a right spirit within, and God restored him and made him whole. God is ready, willing, and able to restore you if you would be willing to humble yourself and repent for your offenses. God's timing is always perfect and good! He promised me a breakthrough before the completion of this book, and I must say that I have received just that! Who knew that God would deliver me through my own words? Well, I guess if it couldn't help me, then how could I ever expect it to help someone else?

I'm grateful for my change because I feel like I'm finally taking a step in the right direction. I may have lost what little street creds that I had from my early days of fighting because I went from *packing a mean punch* to throwing *spiritual windmills*. But I come to serve notice to the enemy that I have the **Undefeated Heavyweight Champion** in my corner and He has yet to lose a fight!

In fact, He informed me that I've been trying to fight my battles long enough and that this battle is no longer mine to fight. So, I'm not worried about the thought of being torn to pieces by my opponent. God has assured me that I'm covered and that I'm worth every battle that He has to fight on my behalf, in order to bring me from victim to victorious! And the same goes for you!

God showed me that He has my back. He stepped in and He renewed my strength! He told me that I have nothing to fear because He's always going to be right there with me. He was there like the *Footprints in the Sand*, carrying me when I could no longer walk for myself. He kept me through my dark days because He has a purpose and a plan for me. Always remember that God has your back and if God is for you, then He's way more than the world against you. Touch your neighbor and tell them, "Your fight is rigged and you were born to win!" We were all born to win, and we will win even with all of our broken pieces because they were necessary to get us to this point! God's Got Your Back!

I pray that I have said something in this book that has helped to set you on the path to your deliverance. I pray that you have gained the strength to repent and renounce any sins of your past in order to be released from that bondage. Satan, I command you to loose here and let us go. You no longer have control over the thoughts in our minds. We're taking back everything that you have tried to steal from us! I declare and decree that as of **TODAY**, our *Pity Party* has turned into our *Praise Party*, and your invitation has been returned to the sender. Satan, you are no longer welcome in my life, you're no longer welcome in my home, and you're no longer welcome in my heart! You've simply got to go!

God wants you to know that you are not your mistakes! You are not your past failures! He's restoring you as you read these words. He's providing a way of escape from the damage of self as we speak! He's doing something new in you at this very moment! I double-dog dare you to reach up and grab EVERYTHING that He has in store for you! It's yours! I declare and decree that you are healed from your brokenness TODAY!

Now unto Him who is able to deliver us from our broken pieces and who is able to keep us from stumbling. To the author and finisher, the founder and perfecter of our faith. To the only wise God, our Saviour. In You, there will be glory and majesty, dominion, and power, both now and forever. In Jesus' name. Amen.

Receive your BREAKTHROUGH!!!

You are no longer BROKEN!!!

You are HEALED!!!

You are FREE!!!

I survived the BROKEN PIECES OF ME... and you can too!

GOD USES BROKEN PEOPLE

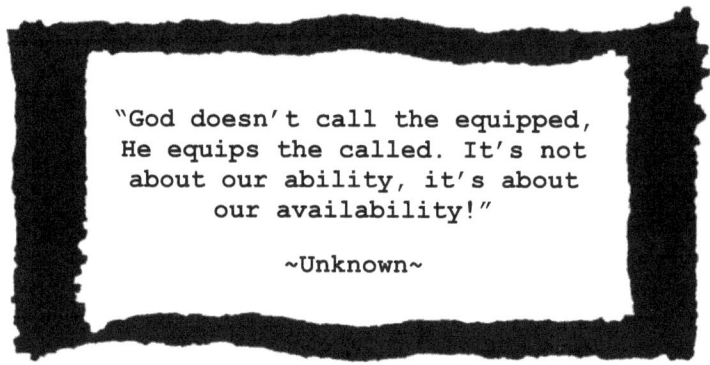

For those of you who think that God can't use you right where you are... think again! Take a look at this list of people that God gladly used to do ministry alongside of Him. Don't be surprised if you find yourself somewhere in this mix.

Noah got drunk - Noah began to be a man of the soil, and he planted a vineyard. He drank of the wine and became drunk and lay uncovered in his tent. **Genesis 9:20-21**

Martha worried - But the Lord answered her, "Martha, Martha, you are anxious and troubled about many things," **Luke 10:41**

Rahab was a prostitute - And they went and came into the house of a prostitute whose name was Rahab and lodged there. **Joshua 2:1**

Naomi was a widow - But Elimelech, the husband of Naomi, died, and she was left with her two sons. **Ruth 1:3**

Leah felt unloved - When the Lord saw that Leah was hated, he opened her womb, but Rachel was barren. And Leah conceived and bore a son, and she called his name Reuben, for she said, "Because the Lord has looked upon my affliction; for now my husband will love me." **Genesis 29:31-32**

Jacob was a trickster - But he said, "Your brother came deceitfully, and he has taken away your blessing." Esau said, "Is he not rightly named Jacob? For he has cheated me these two times. He took away my birthright, and behold, now he has taken away my blessing." **Genesis 27:35-36**

Samson was a womanizer -

- Samson went down to Timnah, and at Timnah he saw one of the daughters of the Philistines. Then he came up and told his father and mother, "I saw one of the daughters of the Philistines at Timnah. Now get her for me as my wife." **Judges 14:1-2**
- Samson went to Gaza, and there he saw a prostitute, and he went in to her. **Judges 16:1**
- After this he loved a woman in the Valley of Sorek, whose name was Delilah. **Judges 16:4**

David was an adulterer - David saw from the roof a woman bathing; and the woman was very beautiful. And David sent and inquired about the woman. And one said, "Is not this Bathsheba, the wife of Uriah the Hittite?" So David sent messengers and took her, and she came to him, and he lay with her. And the woman conceived, and she sent and told David, "I am pregnant." **2 Samuel 11:2-5**

The disciples fell asleep while praying - And he came to the disciples and found them sleeping. And he said to Peter, "So, could you not watch with me one hour?" **Matthew 26:40**

The Samaritan woman was divorced - He said to her, "Go, call your husband and come here." The woman answered and said, "I have no husband." Jesus said to her, "You have correctly said, 'I have no husband'; for you have had five husbands, and the one whom you now have is not your husband; this you have said truly." **John 4:16-18**

Jonah ran from God - The word of the LORD came to Jonah son of Amittai: "Go to the great city of Nineveh and preach against it, because its wickedness has come up before me." But Jonah ran away from the LORD and headed for Tarshish. **Jonah 1:1-3**

Abraham and Sarah were old - Then Abraham fell on his face and laughed and said to himself, "Shall a child be born to a man who is a hundred years old? Shall Sarah, who is ninety years old, bear a child?" **Genesis 17:17**

Zacchaeus was small - He was a chief tax collector and was rich. And he was seeking to see who Jesus was, but on account of the crowd he could not, because he was small in stature. **Luke 19:2-3**

Paul was too religious - Festus said with a loud voice, "Paul, you are out of your mind; your great learning is driving you out of your mind." **Acts 26:24**

A woman had an issue of blood -

- And behold, a woman who had suffered from a discharge of blood for twelve years came up behind him and touched the fringe of his garment. **Matthew 9:20**
- And there was a woman who had had a discharge of blood for twelve years, and who had suffered much under many physicians, and had spent all that she had, and was no better but rather grew worse. **Mark 5:25-26**
- And there was a woman who had had a discharge of blood for twelve years, and though she had spent all her living on physicians, she could not be healed by anyone. **Luke 8:43**

Lazarus was dead - Six days before the Passover, Jesus therefore came to Bethany, where Lazarus was, whom Jesus had raised from the dead. **John 12:1**

Elijah was suicidal - But he himself went a day's journey into the wilderness and came and sat down under a broom tree. And he asked that he might die, saying, "It is enough; now, O Lord, take away my life, for I am no better than my fathers." **1 Kings 19:4**

Joseph was abandoned and abused –

- So when Joseph came to his brothers, they stripped him of his robe, the robe of many colors that he wore. And they took him and threw him into a pit. The pit was empty; there was no water in it. **Genesis 37:23-24**
- His master's wife cast her eyes on Joseph and said, "Lie with me." But he refused. She called to the men of her household and said to them, "See, he has brought among us a Hebrew to laugh at us. He came in to me to lie with me, and I cried out with a loud voice. **Genesis 39:7-8; 14**

Moses had a speech problem - But Moses said to the Lord, "Oh, my Lord, I am not eloquent, either in the past or since you have spoken to your servant, but I am slow of speech and of tongue." **Exodus 4:10**

Mary Magdalene was demon-possessed - and also some women who had been healed of evil spirits and infirmities: Mary, called Magdalene, from whom seven demons had gone out. **Luke 8:2**

Gideon was fearful - And he said to him, "Please, Lord, how can I save Israel? Behold, my clan is the weakest in Manasseh, and I am the least in my father's house." **Judges 6:15**

Peter denied Jesus –

- "This man also was with him." But he denied it, saying, "Woman, I do not know him."
- "You also are one of them." But Peter said, "Man, I am not."
- "Certainly this man also was with him, for he too is a Galilean." But Peter said, "Man, I do not know what you are talking about." **Luke 22:56-61; Matthew 26:69-75**

Thomas doubted Jesus - Then he said to Thomas, "Put your finger here, and see my hands; and put out your hand, and place it in my side. Do not disbelieve, but believe." Thomas answered him, "My Lord and my God!" Jesus said to him, "Have you believed because you have seen me? Blessed are those who have not seen and yet have believed." – **John 20:27-29**

Job lost everything - And he said, "Naked I came from my mother's womb, and naked shall I return. The Lord gave, and the Lord has taken away. **Job 1:21**

Jeremiah and Timothy were young -

- Then I said, "Ah Lord God! Behold, I do not know how to speak, for I am only a youth." But the Lord said to me, "Do not say, I am too young." **Jeremiah 1:6-7**
- Let no one despise you for your youth, but set the believers an example in speech, in conduct, in love, in faith, in purity. **1 Timothy 4:12**

For all who are in need of grace – But he said to me, "My grace is sufficient for you, for my power is made perfect in weakness." Therefore I will boast all the more gladly of my weaknesses, so that the power of Christ may rest upon me." **2 Corinthians 12:9**

SCRIPTURES ON BROKENNESS

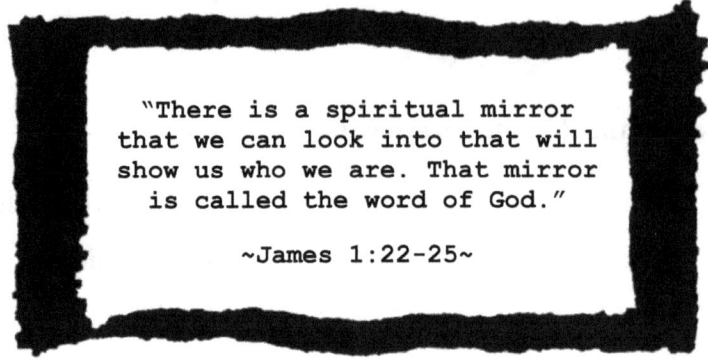

"There is a spiritual mirror that we can look into that will show us who we are. That mirror is called the word of God."

~James 1:22-25~

Psalm 34:18 - The Lord is near to the brokenhearted and saves the crushed in spirit.

Psalm 147:3 - He heals the brokenhearted and binds up their wounds.

Isaiah 41:10 - Fear not, for I am with you; be not dismayed, for I am your God; I will strengthen you, I will help you, I will uphold you with my righteous right hand.

Isaiah 43:2 - When you pass through the waters, I will be with you; and through the rivers, they shall not overwhelm you; when you walk through fire you shall not be burned, and the flame shall not consume you.

Psalm 46:1 - God is our refuge and strength, a very present help in trouble.

Nehemiah 8:10 – And do not be grieved, for the joy of the Lord is your strength.

Romans 8:28 - And we know that for those who love God all things work together for good, for those who are called according to his purpose.

Psalm 51:17 - The sacrifices of God are a broken spirit; a broken and contrite heart, O God, you will not despise.

1 John 1:9 - If we confess our sins, he is faithful and just to forgive us our sins and to cleanse us from all unrighteousness.

John 14:27 - Peace I leave with you; my peace I give to you. Not as the world gives do I give to you. Let not your hearts be troubled, neither let them be afraid.

Psalm 51:10 - Create in me a clean heart, O God, and renew a right spirit within me.

Philippians 4:13 - I can do all things through him who strengthens me.

Matthew 11:28-30 - Come to me, all who labor and are heavy laden, and I will give you rest. Take my yoke upon you, and learn from me, for I am gentle and lowly in heart, and you will find rest for your souls. For my yoke is easy, and my burden is light."

Matthew 5:4 - Blessed are those who mourn, for they shall be comforted.

Joshua 1:9 - Have I not commanded you? Be strong and courageous. Do not be frightened, and do not be dismayed, for the Lord your God is with you wherever you go.

1 Peter 5:7 - Casting all your anxieties on him, because he cares for you.

1 Peter 5:10 - And after you have suffered a little while, the God of all grace, who has called you to his eternal glory in Christ, will himself restore, confirm, strengthen, and establish you.

Psalm 34:17 - When the righteous cry for help, the Lord hears and delivers them out of all their troubles.

Philippians 1:6 - And I am sure of this, that he who began a good work in you will bring it to completion at the day of Jesus Christ.

About the Author

Kimbria is a native of Memphis, TN. She earned her Associate in Biblical Studies from Memphis Center of Urban Theological Studies (MCUTS) at Lancaster Bible College and is currently pursuing her Bachelor of Entrepreneurial Leadership from MCUTS at Union University. Kimbria is a licensed and ordained reverend at Redemption Church, located in Memphis, TN., under the leadership of Pastors Devin & Samantha Westbrook. She loves music, enjoys spending time with her family, and is just happy to serve wherever she is needed. Kimbria truly believes to be in ministry, you must have the heart to serve and not just serve, but serve with gladness.

www.ingramcontent.com/pod-product-compliance
Lightning Source LLC
Chambersburg PA
CBHW060416050426
42449CB00009B/1989